T0380811

CHANGED BY HIS AMAZING Grace

Student Companion
Workbook

DR. MOREINE FONTENELLE

WESTBOW
PRESS®
A DIVISION OF THOMAS NELSON
& ZONDERVAN

This book is a work of non-fiction. Unless otherwise noted, the author and the publisher make no explicit guarantees as to the accuracy of the information contained in this book and in some cases, names of people and places have been altered to protect their privacy.

WestBow Press books may be ordered through booksellers or by contacting:

WestBow Press
A Division of Thomas Nelson & Zondervan
1663 Liberty Drive
Bloomington, IN 47403
www.westbowpress.com
844-714-3454

Scripture quotations marked (NLT) are taken from the Holy Bible, New Living Translation, copyright ©1996, 2004, 2015 by Tyndale House Foundation. Used by permission of Tyndale House Publishers, a Division of Tyndale House Ministries, Carol Stream, Illinois 60188. All rights reserved.

ISBN: 979-8-3850-4733-8 (sc)
ISBN: 979-8-3850-4732-1 (e)

Print information available on the last page.

WestBow Press rev. date: 04/08/2025

CONTENTS

STUDENT COMPANION WORKBOOK

Purpose of the Workbook

This Student Companion Workbook is designed to deepen your understanding of grace through reflective journaling, practical exercises, and meaningful group discussions. Aligned with the theme of 'Changed by His Amazing Grace,' this workbook invites you to actively engage with the transformative power of grace in your life and community.

How to Use the Workbook

Each chapter includes prayer prompts, blessings, practical application and discussion questions, journey tracker, and personal reflections to guide you on your journey of transformation through grace.

Prayer Prompts: Dedicate time to reflect on the prayers, blessings, and application questions provided in each chapter. Use this workbook during your devotional time or as part of a group study. Begin each chapter by centering your heart through prayer.

Chapter Overview: This overview is taken directly from the book *Changed by His Amazing Grace,* Author: Dr. Moreine Fontenelle

Key Memory Verse: Use this section to memorize key scriptures and reflect on their personal application.

Group Discussion Questions: These questions are designed to foster meaningful discussions in a group setting. Use them to explore themes of grace, forgiveness, and community. Foster meaningful conversations with others to deepen understanding.

Practical Applications: Take actionable steps to incorporate grace into your daily life. This section includes actionable steps to help you apply the principles of grace in your life and relationships.

Grace Journey Tracker: Use the tracker to log your daily or weekly reflections, prayers, and actions related to living out grace. This tool will help you see patterns of growth and identify areas where you need more grace.

Artistic Reflection: Express your thoughts and feelings creatively. Be honest and open as you explore how grace is at work in your life.

Personal Growth: Revisit chapters and sections that resonate with you as your understanding of grace deepens over time. Summarize your insights and commit to living out grace

Blessings: Proclaim the word of God in and over your life.

Session 1
WHY GRACE MATTERS

Lesson Objectives

By the end of this lesson, readers should be able to:

- **Understand the foundational role of grace** in salvation and the Christian life.
- **Distinguish between grace and the law**, recognizing that grace is a gift, not something earned.
- **Identify personal areas where grace has impacted their life** and where they need to embrace it more fully.
- **Recognize how grace sustains and transforms**, not just at salvation but in everyday struggles.
- **Develop a deeper gratitude for God's grace**, leading to a life of faith and reliance on Him rather than human effort.

<u>OPEN</u>

Leader: Open the session with prayer. If your group is brand new or if everyone doesn't know each other well, spend time getting to know each other before asking the opening question.

Prayer

"Lord, thank You for Your amazing grace that changes lives. Open my heart to receive Your grace more fully and transform me through it. Help me to see Your hand at work in every area of my life. Amen."

Opening Question: "Can you remember a time when you received an unexpected gift? How did it make you feel? Now, thinking about salvation as God's gift of grace, how does that comparison help you understand what it means to be 'born again'?"

Chapter 1 Overview

Grace is at the very heart of the Christian faith. It is God's unmerited favor, freely given to humanity through Jesus Christ. This chapter explores why grace is essential, how it transforms lives, and how it serves as the foundation of salvation and spiritual growth. It contrasts grace with the law, emphasizing that while the law reveals sin, only grace offers redemption.

God's grace not only saves but also sustains and transforms believers, calling them into a deeper relationship with Him. Grace allows us to stand in our true identity as loved, forgiven, and redeemed children of God, free from striving and performance-based faith.

Key Memory Verse

Ephesians 2:8-9 (NLT) – *"God saved you by his grace when you believed. And you can't take credit for this; it is a gift from God. Salvation is not a reward for the good things we have done, so none of us can boast about it."*

GROUP DISCUSSION – *Understanding and Living Grace*

1. How would you explain the concept of grace to someone who has never encountered it?

2. Why is it important to understand grace as a gift rather than something earned?

3. How does grace differ from the concept of mercy? What role do both play in our spiritual journey?

4. What is the significance of **spiritual birth** in the life of a believer?

5. According to **Romans 3:20-24**, what role does the law play in leading us to grace?

6. What does **2 Corinthians 5:21** reveal about Jesus' role in restoring our relationship with God?

7. How do the Hebrew word **hesed** and the Greek word **charis** deepen our understanding of grace?

8. What makes grace the distinguishing factor between Christianity and other belief systems?

9. How is grace described as a **bridge** between humanity's sin and God's holiness?

10. How would you explain the concept of grace to someone who has never heard about it?

11. The chapter describes grace as the **heartbeat** of the Christian journey. Why is it essential for both salvation and daily living?

12. How does the world's approach to success and earning compare to God's approach to grace?

13. The chapter emphasizes that grace not only forgives but **transforms**. What does this transformation look like in a believer's life?

14. How can we, as a **faith community**, ensure that grace is central to how we interact with one another?

15. In what practical ways can we extend grace to others—especially those who may not seem to deserve it?

16. The chapter states that **grace sustains** us in daily life. Can you share an example of a time when grace gave you strength in a difficult situation?

17. The chapter mentions that grace calls us out of **shame and striving**. Have you ever struggled with feeling unworthy of grace? How did you overcome it?

18. What does it mean to **rest in grace** rather than striving to earn God's approval?

19. How has your understanding of grace changed as you have grown in your faith?

PRACTICAL APPLICATION QUESTIONS - *Experiencing Grace*

1. Can you identify a **specific moment** in your life when you truly experienced God's grace? How did it impact you?

2. What practical steps can you take this week to embrace grace in an area of your life where you feel stuck or discouraged?

3. The testimony in this chapter describes a moment of encountering grace in a time of brokenness. Have you had a similar experience? How did it change you?

4. What does it mean to you personally that God's grace is both a gift and a transformative force?

GRACE JOURNEY TRACKER

Use the tracker below to log your reflections, prayers, and acts of grace: Focus on key events, blessings, or turning points influenced by grace.

Date	Acts of Grace Showed	How I Experience Grace	Areas for More Grace

Artistic Reflection

Take a moment to express your understanding of grace creatively. Sketch, journal, or write a poem that captures what grace means to you.

PERSONAL GROWTH

Summarize your insights from this chapter. What have you learned about grace, and how do you plan to apply it in your life moving forward?

Pray for understanding of God's grace and ask Him to reveal specific moments of grace in your life. Record your prayer here.

Extend Grace: Identify someone in your life who needs grace—whether through forgiveness, encouragement, or patience. Take a step this week to extend that grace to them.

Memorize Scripture: Choose one of the key verses from this chapter (e.g., Ephesians 2:8-9 or 2 Corinthians 5:21) and meditate on its meaning throughout the week.

Prayer Time: Spend time thanking God for His grace. Ask Him to reveal areas where you need to surrender and receive more of His grace.

BLESSING

May you find yourself enveloped in the presence of God. May you feel His gaze upon you and His peace surrounding you. May you encounter His life-changing presence and tranquility, leading you toward total well-being.

Session 2

THE JOURNEY TO REDEMPTION

Lesson Objectives

By the end of this lesson, readers should be able to:

- **Understand redemption as God's ultimate act of grace** and how it brings spiritual freedom.
- **Recognize that redemption is a process**, requiring daily reliance on God's grace.
- **Reflect on their own journey of redemption**, identifying ways God has rescued and restored them.
- **Learn to trust in God's redemptive work** even in moments of struggle or failure.
- **Develop a deeper appreciation for Jesus' sacrifice**, leading to a life of gratitude and obedience.

<u>OPEN</u>

Leader: Open the session with prayer. If your group is brand new or if everyone doesn't know each other well, spend time getting to know each other before asking the opening question.

Prayer

"Lord, I invite Your grace to transform me from the inside out. Change my heart, renew my mind, and align my actions with Your will. Help me to reflect Your love in all I do. Amen."

Opening Question: "Can you think of a time in your life when you felt stuck, hopeless, or burdened by something you couldn't fix on your own? What helped you find hope or a way forward? How does this relate to the way God's grace works in our journey to redemption?"

Chapter Overview

Redemption is at the core of God's plan for humanity. This chapter explores how grace not only saves but also restores and transforms lives. The journey to redemption is not just about receiving salvation; it is about walking daily in the freedom and renewal that grace provides.

Through real-life testimonies like Clayvon's breakthrough, readers witness the power of surrendering to God's grace. The chapter emphasizes how redemption is not only about forgiveness but also about transformation, renewal, and community restoration. As we grow spiritually, we learn to embrace grace fully, allowing it to reshape our attitudes, relationships, and purpose.

Through Christ's sacrifice, believers are reconciled to God and invited into a new way of living. The chapter highlights how redemption is not earned but is a gift of grace, paid for by the blood of Jesus. It also emphasizes that accepting this grace leads to transformation—a shift in identity, mindset, and purpose.

Key Memory Verse

1 Peter 2:2 (NLT) – *"Like newborn babies, you must crave pure spiritual milk so that you will grow into a full experience of salvation."*

GROUP DISCUSSION QUESTIONS - *Understanding & Living Redemption*

1. What does redemption mean to you personally?

2. How does understanding God's grace through redemption change the way you see yourself?

3. What does 1 Peter 1:18-19 teach us about the **cost of redemption**?

4. How does **Ephesians 1:7** explain the relationship between grace and redemption?

5. What role does grace play in transforming our past brokenness into wholeness in Christ?

6. How does **Romans 6:14** describe the freedom we have in Christ?

7. What does the story of the woman caught in adultery (John 8:1-11) teach us about Jesus' response to sin and redemption?

8. How does grace work both **personally and within the faith community**?

9. What does Colossians 3:13 teach us about grace and forgiveness in relationships?

10. How does Clayvon's testimony highlight the transformative power of grace?

11. What are some ways we can encourage spiritual growth in new believers?

12. What is the relationship between forgiveness and grace, and why is it essential for building a **Christ-centered community**?

13. How do we ensure that we extend the same grace to others that God has shown to us?

14. How do personal experiences of grace and redemption impact on our testimony to others?

15. How does understanding grace change the way we respond to our own failures and those of others?

16. How can believers model Jesus' grace and forgiveness in their daily interactions?

PRACTICAL APPLICATION QUESTIONS - *Experiencing Grace*

1. Where in your life have you seen the transforming power of grace at work?

2. Are there areas where you are still conforming to the world's patterns? How can grace help **renew your mind**?

3. Clayvon struggled with anger and despair before encountering grace. Can you relate to a time when you wrestled with negative emotions? How did God's grace help you **overcome**?

4. How has God's grace brought healing and restoration to your personal relationships?

5. In what ways do you see yourself growing spiritually, as described in 1 Peter 2:2?

6. Redemption is not just about salvation but also daily renewal. How can you rely on grace to help you overcome current struggles?

7. What does "neither do I condemn you" (John 8:11) mean in your life today?

GRACE JOURNEY TRACKER

Use the tracker below to log your reflections, prayers, and acts of grace: How do you personally apply the concept of redemption in your daily life?

DATE	ACTS OF GRACE SHOWED	HOW I EXPERIENCE GRACE	AREAS FOR MORE GRACE

Artistic Reflection

Reflect on the concept of redemption. Create a visual or written piece that illustrates what it means to be redeemed by grace.

PERSONAL GROWTH

1. **Reflect & Journal:** Write about a time when you felt **redeemed**. How did God's grace play a part in this transformation?

2. **Memorize key scripture:** Focus on Ephesians 1:7, Titus 2:14 and Romans 6:14. Reflect on them throughout the week and meditate on how grace brings freedom.

3. **Extend Grace:** Identify a person who needs forgiveness or encouragement. Take a practical step toward reconciliation.

4. Daily Grace Practice: Each day, find a way to extend grace—whether in words, actions, or forgiveness.

BLESSING

May the Lord's right-hand support you according to His word. May His gentleness make you great and give you a wide place for your steps so that your feet do not slip.

Session 3

THE GRACE OF GOD - REDEMPTION'S SONG

Lesson Objectives

By the end of this lesson, readers should be able to:

- **Understanding grace as the ongoing song of redemption**, not just a moment of salvation.
- **Recognize that God's grace meets them in their failures** and offers restoration. **Identify personal areas where they need to embrace grace** instead of guilt or shame.
- **Develop a renewed confidence in their identity in Christ**, knowing they are fully forgiven and redeemed.
- **Commit to living out grace** by extending forgiveness and love to others.

<u>OPEN</u>

Leader: Open the session with prayer. Ask if there are any questions from the previous session.

Prayer

"Lord, I invite Your grace to transform me from the inside out. Change my heart, renew my mind, and align my actions with Your will. Help me to reflect Your love in all I do. Amen."

Opening Question: "Think about a time when you felt unworthy of love or forgiveness. How did that experience shape your view of yourself and others? How might understanding God's grace change the way you see those moments?"

Chapter Overview

Grace is the song of redemption that echoes throughout Scripture and our lives. This chapter highlights how grace is not just a one-time gift but a continuous melody that transforms, restores, and sustains believers. God's grace meets us in our brokenness, lifts us from despair, and sets us on a path of renewal.

Through personal testimonies like Aisha's journey, we see how God's grace restores brokenness, heals relationships, and draws people back to Him. The Prodigal Son's story illustrates God's unrelenting love, showing how He meets us in our failures with open arms. Redemption is not just about forgiveness—it is a complete transformation that allows believers to step into a new identity in Christ.

Using biblical examples and testimonies, the chapter illustrates that grace is not based on human merit but on God's unchanging love. The story of the Prodigal Son serves as a reminder that God doesn't just forgive—He fully restores. Grace is the invitation to live in the freedom of redemption and to let God's love reshape our identity.

Key Memory Verse

Ephesians 1:7 (NLT) – *"He is so rich in kindness and grace that he purchased our freedom with the blood of his Son and forgave our sins."*

GROUP DISCUSSION QUESTIONS - *Understanding and Living Grace*

1. What does redemption mean to you personally?

2. How does understanding God's grace through redemption change the way you see yourself?

3. How does **Exodus 34:6-7** describe God's character and His grace?

4. What does **Ephesians 2:8** reveal about salvation through grace?

5. Why is grace referred to as **redemption's song** in this chapter?

6. What does Isaiah 53:5-6 teach us about the cost of grace?

7. How does the story of the **Prodigal Son** (Luke 15:11-32) illustrate the depth of God's grace?

8. What does **Romans 3:23-24** say about the universal reach of grace?

9. How does 2 Corinthians 5:17 describe the transformation that occurs through redemption?

10. The chapter emphasizes that **grace is not just about forgiveness but transformation.** What does that look like in a believer's life?

11. How does understanding that **grace is a gift** impact the way we interact with others?

12. What are some ways the church can be a **reflection of grace** to people who feel unworthy?

13. The **Prodigal Son's father ran to him** instead of condemning him. How does this shape our understanding of God's response to us when we fail?

14. What does **1 Peter 3:15** teach us about sharing our testimony of grace with others?

15. How can we model **Jesus' grace and forgiveness** in our daily interactions?

16. How can we intentionally remind ourselves of **God's redeeming grace** during difficult seasons?

PRACTICAL APPLICATION QUESTIONS - *Experiencing Grace*

1. Where in your life have you seen the transforming power of grace at work?

2. Are there areas where you are still conforming to the world's patterns? How can grace help renew your mind?

3. Aisha struggled with **shame and unworthiness** before encountering grace. Can you relate to a time when you felt distant from God? How did grace bring you back?

4. How has understanding **God's unconditional love** changed the way you view your past mistakes?

5. What are some practical ways you can apply **Romans 5:1-2** to walk in the peace of God's grace?

6. In what areas of your life do you need to stop striving and **rest in God's grace**?

7. How does the realization that Jesus **paid the ultimate price for your redemption** impact your daily choices?

8. If God's grace transforms us, what specific areas of your life have been reshaped by His love?

GRACE JOURNEY TRACKER

Use the tracker below to log your reflections, prayers, and acts of grace:

Date	Acts of Grace Showed	How I Experience Grace	Areas for More Grace

Artistic Reflection

Reflect on the concept of redemption. Create a visual or written piece that illustrates what it means to be redeemed by grace.

PERSONAL GROWTH

What new perspective on redemption have you gained? How will you live differently because of it?

Reflect & Journal: Write about a time when God's redemptive grace lifted you out of despair. How did it change your outlook?

Extend Grace: Identify someone in your life who needs forgiveness or encouragement. Take a step to extend grace toward them.

Memorize Scripture: Focus on **Isaiah 1:18** or **Ephesians 2:8-9** and meditate on how grace cleanses and transforms us.

Daily Grace Practice: Make it a habit to **extend kindness, patience, and forgiveness** in a way that reflects God's grace.

BLESSING

May the Lord's right-hand support you according to His word. May His gentleness make you great and give you a wide place for your steps so that your feet do not slip.

Session 4

WALKING IN TRANSFORMATION

Lesson Objectives

By the end of this lesson, readers should be able to:

- **Understand that transformation is a process**, requiring faith, surrender, and trust in God's timing.
- **Recognize the difference between self-improvement and true spiritual transformation** through grace.
- **Identify areas in their lives where they need to trust God's process**, even when they don't see immediate results.
- **Develop a mindset that aligns with God's truth**, rejecting worldly patterns of thinking.
- **Commit to walking in obedience and faith**, knowing that transformation happens through daily surrender.

OPEN

Leader: Open the session with prayer. Ask if there are any questions from the previous session.

DR. MOREINE FONTENELLE

Prayer

"Father God, Thank You for giving us a new identity in Christ. Help us to see ourselves the way You see us—loved, chosen, and redeemed. May we walk confidently in this new identity, knowing that we are no longer defined by our past but by Your grace. Remind us daily of who we are in You. In Jesus' name, Amen."

Opening Question: "Can you recall a time when God was leading you into transformation, but you resisted because it felt too difficult or uncertain? What helped you finally trust Him in that season?"

Chapter Overview

Transformation is an ongoing journey that requires trust in God's grace. This chapter explores how believers are called to walk in faith, even when they do not fully understand God's plans. True transformation is not just about behavior change but about a renewed mind and heart, shaped by God's grace.

We are called to walk in grace, learning obedience, sacrifice, and faith. The transformation process is not instant but an ongoing journey that requires surrender to God's will. Through biblical examples such as Paul's conversion, and Jeremiah's imagery of the potter and the clay, we see how God molds us to reflect His purpose. Transformation is fueled by grace and sustained by faith, leading us to become new creations in Christ.

Using the example of Paul's radical transformation, the chapter highlights that God's grace not only saves but also empowers believers to live differently. It challenges readers to surrender their doubts, fears, and struggles to God, trusting Him to complete the work He has begun in them.

Key Memory Verse

Romans 12:2 (NLT) – *"Don't copy the behavior and customs of this world, but let God transform you into a new person by changing the way you think. Then you will learn to know God's will for you, which is good and pleasing and perfect."*

GROUP DISCUSSION QUESTIONS - *Understanding and Living Transformed*

1. What does it mean to you to be a "new creation" in Christ?

2. How has transformation through grace impacted your daily life?

3. How does God's grace work in us to renew our minds and guard our hearts? Consider ways you can actively participate in God's transforming work in your life, such as through prayer, scripture, or serving others.

4. What does **Luke 9:23** teach us about discipleship and transformation?

5. How does **Acts 9:1-19** illustrate the immediate yet ongoing nature of transformation?

6. What does **Jeremiah 18:1-6** teach about God's role as the potter in our lives?

7. According to **Romans 5:1-2**, how do grace and faith work together in transformation?

8. What does **2 Corinthians 5:17** mean when it says believers become a "new creation"?

9. How does **Philippians 1:6** assure us that transformation is a continuous work of God?

10. How does **Isaiah 41:10** encourage us when we feel weak in our transformation journey?

11. What are some obstacles that prevent believers from fully surrendering to God's transformation?

12. How can the **analogy of the butterfly's transformation** help us understand spiritual growth?

13. What does it mean to take up your cross **daily** as Jesus commands in **Luke 9:23**?

14. How does trusting God **beyond our understanding** impact how we handle life's uncertainties?

15. What role does the **faith community** play in encouraging transformation?

16. How does **James 2:14-26** emphasize the connection between faith and action?

17. How can we actively model God's grace to others who are struggling in their transformation?

PRACTICAL APPLICATION QUESTIONS - *Experiencing Grace in Transformation*

1. In what ways do you rely on your own strength instead of approaching God's throne of grace?

2. How can you remind yourself to seek God's grace in moments of weakness or fear?

3. Transformation is a process. Can you think of a time when you struggled with old habits or doubts? How did you experience God's grace in those moments?

4. How has God used challenges in your life to shape and refine you?

5. What does trusting God "beyond our understanding" look like in your personal faith journey?

6. Have you ever felt **unworthy of transformation**? How does God's grace reassure you?

7. In what ways has **faith helped sustain you** when transformation felt difficult?

8. How does recognizing that transformation is a **lifelong process** change your perspective on spiritual growth?

GRACE JOURNEY TRACKER

Use the tracker below to log your reflections, prayers, and acts of grace:

Date	Acts of Grace Showed	How I Experience Grace	Areas for More Grace

Artistic Reflection

Create an artistic expression of transformation. Use words or imagery to represent the journey from old to new in Christ.

PERSONAL GROWTH

Summarize your insights from this chapter. How has understanding grace-driven transformation impacted your faith?

Write about a specific area of your life that has changed. Thank God for His transforming grace in your life and pray for continued change. Ask For strength to grow and reflect more on Him.

Reflect & Journal: Write about a time when trusting God required faith beyond your understanding. What did you learn?

Commit to Obedience: Choose one area of your life where you need to surrender more fully to God's transformation. Pray over it and take a step of faith this week.

Memorize Scripture: Focus on 2 Corinthians 12:9 or Philippians 1:6 and meditate on how God's grace sustains us in weakness.

Daily Grace Practice: Intentionally choose to show grace to someone in need of patience, forgiveness, or encouragement.

BLESSING

May you be rooted and grounded in your identity in Christ. May the truth of who you are in God's eyes bring you peace and confidence today and always.

Session 5

GRACE FOR THE BROKEN

Lesson Objectives

By the end of this lesson, readers should be able to:

- **Recognize that brokenness is not the end** but the beginning of God's restorative work.
- **Understand that God sees and responds to their pain**, just as He did for Elijah and Hagar.
- **Identify areas where they need healing and restoration** and invite God into those spaces.
- **Learn to depend on the Holy Spirit** as the source of renewal and strength.
- **Develop a deeper trust in God's plan**, even when life feels broken and uncertain.

OPEN

Leader: Open the session with prayer. Ask if there are any questions from the previous session.

Prayer

"Father, help me to trust in Your love and grace to heal my brokenness. Restore my spirit, renew my hope, and guide me toward Your purpose. In Jesus' name, Amen."

Opening Question: "Can you think of a time when you felt completely broken—whether through loss, failure, or personal struggles? In that moment, how did you experience God's grace, or how do you wish you had?"

Chapter Overview

God's grace is most evident in our moments of deepest brokenness. This chapter explores how His love reaches into the shattered places of our lives, offering healing, restoration, and hope. It reassures readers that no matter their past mistakes or current struggles, God's grace is sufficient.

We explore how trials refine our character and deepen our trust in God. Through biblical accounts like Elijah's despair (1 Kings 19:4-8) and Hagar's encounter with God (Genesis 16), we see how the Father, Son, and Holy Spirit work to restore, heal, transform lives, and redeems the brokenhearted. It also emphasizes the role of the Father, Son, and Holy Spirit in bringing complete restoration through justification, sanctification, and glorification, ensuring that God's grace is sufficient for every moment of brokenness.

Key Memory Verse

Psalm 34:18 (NLT) – *"The Lord is close to the brokenhearted; he rescues those whose spirits are crushed."*

GROUP DISCUSSION QUESTIONS - *Understanding and Living Grace in Brokenness*

1. How has God's grace brought restoration in your life or the lives of others you know?

2. What does it mean to trust God's grace in moments of brokenness?

3. How does **2 Corinthians 12:9** encourage us to rely on grace during times of weakness?

4. What does **James 1:2-3** teach about trials and endurance?

5. How did God restore **Elijah in 1 Kings 19:4-8**, and what does this teach about His grace?

6. What does the name **El Roi** (Genesis 16) reveal about God's nature?

7. How does **Romans 8:28** assure us that God works through our brokenness for good?

8. What are the three theological stages of transformation (**justification, sanctification, glorification**) and how do they shape our faith journey?

9. How does **Psalm 34:18** describe God's heart for the brokenhearted?

10. How does the story of **the woman with the issue of blood** (**Mark 5:25-34**) illustrate God's restoring grace?

11. What can we learn from **Hagar's encounter with God in the wilderness**?

12. What role does **faith-based communities** play in healing from brokenness?

13. How does the Holy Spirit intercede for us in times of weakness (**Romans 8:26-27**)?

14. What does it mean to **exchange our ashes for beauty** as described in **Isaiah 61:1**?

15. How can we model **grace and compassion** toward those who are struggling?

16. Why is it important to remember that **God does not waste our brokenness**?

PRACTICAL APPLICATION QUESTIONS

1. What areas of your life feel most broken? How can you invite God's grace into those spaces?

2. Think about a time when God restored you. How did His grace bring healing and hope?

3. Have you ever experienced a season where you felt broken beyond repair? How did you encounter God's grace in that time?

4. What does it mean for you to **invite God into your brokenness**?

5. How does recognizing that God is close to the brokenhearted change your perspective on suffering?

6. What steps can you take to **trust God's plan even in times of uncertainty?**

7. Have you struggled to forgive yourself for past failures? How does grace help you let go?

8. What areas of your life do you need to surrender to God for healing?

GRACE JOURNEY TRACKER

Use the tracker below to log your reflections, prayers, and acts of grace:

DATE	ACTS OF GRACE SHOWED	HOW I EXPERIENCE GRACE	AREAS FOR MORE GRACE

Artistic Reflection

Create a visual or written piece that represents how God's grace has healed your brokenness.

PERSONAL GROWTH

Summarize your journey of healing through grace. What have you learned, and how will you continue to seek God's grace in broken areas of your life?

Reflect & Journal: Write about a time when **God met you in your brokenness**. How did He bring healing or hope?

Extend Grace: Identify someone who is struggling and reach out with **words of encouragement or acts of kindness**.

Memorize Scripture: Meditate on **Psalm 34:18 or 2 Corinthians 12:9**, reminding yourself of God's nearness in hardship.

Daily Grace Practice: Choose to extend grace **to yourself** by letting go of past regrets and embracing God's love for you.

BLESSING

May God's grace be your refuge and strength in times of brokenness. May you find comfort in His presence and healing through His love. May you rise from your brokenness renewed and ready to walk in His calling.

Session 6

OVERCOMING TRIALS – STRENGTH IN HIS PRESENCE

Lesson Objectives

By the end of this lesson, readers should be able to:

- **Recognize that trials are part of the Christian journey** and can lead to spiritual growth.
- **Understand that God's grace is sufficient** and that His power is revealed in times of weakness.
- **Develop perseverance and faith** by trusting in God's presence, even when facing challenges.
- **Learn how to shift their mindset**, seeing trials as opportunities to deepen their trust in God.
- **Apply biblical strategies to overcome trials**, such as prayer, scripture meditation, and community support.

<u>OPEN</u>

Leader: Open the session with prayer. Ask if there are any questions from the previous session.

Prayer

"Heavenly Father, thank You for the strength You give us through Your grace, especially in times of trial. Help us to trust in Your grace when we face hardship, knowing that You are always with us. In Jesus' name, Amen."

Opening Question: "Think about a time when you faced a trial or hardship. In that moment, did you find it easy or difficult to trust in God's presence? How did that experience shape your faith?"

Chapter Overview

Trials and hardships are a part of life, but God's grace provides the strength to endure them. This chapter explores how believers can find peace and perseverance in difficult times by leaning on God's presence. It emphasizes that trials are not meant to break us but to refine us, strengthen our faith, and draw us closer to God.

Through personal devotion, prayer, and Scripture, we learn to rely on God's grace as strength in weakness (2 Corinthians 12:9). Trials are not signs of God's absence but opportunities for His grace to be revealed. Sanctification through suffering refines our faith, making us more like Christ. Jesus, our ultimate example, endured hardship for the joy set before Him, teaching us that God's presence sustains us through every storm.

Through biblical examples like Paul's endurance through suffering and Job's unwavering faith, this chapter highlights how God sustains His people in the midst of challenges. It encourages believers to shift their perspective—seeing trials as opportunities for spiritual growth rather than obstacles to faith.

Key Memory Verse

2 Corinthians 12:9 (NLT) – *"Each time he said, 'My grace is all you need. My power works best in weakness.' So now I am glad to boast about my weaknesses, so that the power of Christ can work through me."*

GROUP DISCUSSION QUESTIONS - *Understanding Trials & God's Presence*

1. Share a time when you experienced God's grace in a trial. How did it change your perspective?

2. How can we encourage others to trust in God's grace during hardships?

3. How does **James 1:2-4** describe the purpose of trials in our faith journey?

4. What does **Psalm 23:4** reveal about God's presence during difficult times?

5. How does **2 Corinthians 12:9** encourage us to trust God's grace in weakness?

6. What does **1 Peter 5:10** teach about God's restoration after suffering?

7. How does **Joshua 1:9** reassure us of God's presence in every circumstance?

8. Why does **Hebrews 12:2** call us to look to Jesus as our model for enduring trials?

9. What role does the Holy Spirit play as **the Comforter (John 14:26)** during hardships?

10. Why is **trusting God beyond our understanding** an important part of overcoming trials?

11. How do **Romans 8:28** and **2 Corinthians 4:17** shape our understanding of suffering?

12. How does Christ's response in **Gethsemane (Matthew 26:36-39)** model surrender in trials?

13. How can we encourage others who are struggling with their faith during difficult times?

14. What does it mean to **rejoice in trials** while acknowledging the pain they bring?

15. How can focusing on **eternity (Revelation 21:4)** provide hope in moments of suffering?

16. What are some practical ways to remain steadfast in faith when facing hardship?

PRACTICAL APPLICATION QUESTIONS

1. How has God's grace helped you endure difficult times in the past?

2. What does it mean to you to trust that His grace is sufficient for every challenge?

3. Have you ever experienced a time when you felt abandoned by God? How did His grace sustain you?

4. How does recognizing trials as opportunities for spiritual growth change your perspective on suffering?

5. What past struggles have strengthened your trust in God's presence and faithfulness?

6. How can you remind yourself of **God's sufficient grace** in your current trials?

7. What lessons from Jesus' suffering on the cross encourage you to endure hardship with faith?

8. How do you see **sanctification at work** in your life through difficult seasons?

GRACE JOURNEY TRACKER

Use the tracker below to log your reflections, prayers, and acts of grace:

DATE	ACTS OF GRACE SHOWED	HOW I EXPERIENCE GRACE	AREAS FOR MORE GRACE

Artistic Reflection

Illustrate or write about a storm or trial in your life and how God's grace brought you peace and strength.

PERSONAL GROWTH

Reflect & Journal: Write about a trial where God's presence sustained you. How did it shape your faith?

Journal your experiences and how God's grace shaped your actions. For one week, consciously reflect grace in every interaction you have.

Commit to Trust: Choose a challenging area in your life where you will intentionally surrender to God's grace this week.

Memorize Scripture: Meditate on Psalm 23:4 or James 1:2-3 to remind yourself of God's nearness in trials.

Encourage Others: Identify someone facing hardship and offer words of encouragement or practical support.

BLESSING

May God's grace sustain you through every trial. May you find strength in His presence and peace in His promises, no matter the circumstances.

Session 7

LIVING OVERFLOWING OF GRACE

Lesson Objectives

By the end of this lesson, readers should be able to:

- **Understand that grace is abundant** and meant to be shared, not just received.
- **Recognize the connection between grace and joy,** learning how a grace-filled life brings peace.
- **Identify areas in their lives where they can reflect God's grace,** whether in relationships, workplace, or ministry.
- **Learn how to live with gratitude and generosity,** responding to grace by extending kindness and forgiveness to others.
- **Embrace a daily walk with the Holy Spirit**, allowing His grace to continually renew and refresh them.

<u>OPEN</u>

Leader: Open the session with prayer. Ask if there are any questions from the previous session.

Prayer

"Lord, let Your grace overflow in my life so that it may touch and bless others. Help me to share the abundance of Your love and grace with those around me. Amen."

Opening Question: "Think about a time when someone showed you unexpected grace—whether through forgiveness, kindness, or generosity. How did that experience impact you, and how did it shape the way you now extend grace to others?"

Chapter Overview

This chapter focuses on Living Overflowing Grace—sharing God's love with others through unity, service, and forgiveness. God's grace is not meant to be kept to ourselves—it is meant to overflow into every aspect of our lives and impact those around us. Believers are called to actively extend grace in relationships, becoming vessels of God's transformative love. Through Christ's example and the work of the Holy Spirit, we are empowered to forgive, serve, and uplift others.

This chapter explores how believers can live in the abundance of grace, allowing it to shape their attitudes, relationships, and daily experiences. Living in grace brings joy, peace, and a steadfast faith, even in uncertain times.

Through Jesus' teaching in John 7:38, believers are called to be streams of living water, sharing the grace they have received. This chapter encourages readers to reflect on the ways grace has transformed them and to seek opportunities to extend that same grace to others.

Key Memory Verse

John 7:38 (NLT) – *"Anyone who believes in me may come and drink! For the Scriptures declare, 'Rivers of living water will flow from his heart.'"*

GROUP DISCUSSION QUESTIONS - *Understanding Overflowing Grace*

1. What does it mean to live a life of overflow through grace?

2. How can the overflow of God's grace impact your relationships and community?

3. How does **1 John 4:19** explain the source of our love for others?

4. What does **Romans 5:8** reveal about the cost of grace?

5. How does **John 8:1-11** demonstrate Jesus' grace toward the broken?

6. In **John 13:1-17**, what lesson does Jesus teach through washing the disciples' feet?

7. How does **Ephesians 2:7** point toward God's **ultimate redemptive plan**?

8. What does **John 15:5** teach about remaining in Christ to live out grace?

9. Why is grace both **a gift and a responsibility** for believers?

10. How does **God's grace empower believers** to live differently than the world?

11. What role does the Holy Spirit **(Romans 5:5)** play in helping us extend grace?

12. How do **Galatians 5:22-23** and the fruits of the Spirit reflect God's grace in action?

13. How can we encourage **grace-centered conversations** in our homes and churches?

14. What barriers keep us from showing grace, and how can we overcome them?

15. How does living a **grace-filled life** impact our witness to the world?

16. Why does Jesus tell Peter to forgive **seventy times seven (Matthew 18:21-22)**?

PRACTICAL APPLICATION QUESTIONS

1. How has God's grace overflowed in your life, blessing others?

2. In what ways can you share His grace with your family, friends, and community?

3. Who in your life needs grace right now, and how can you extend it?

4. Have you ever struggled with forgiving someone? What did God teach you through it?

5. How does understanding the **cost of grace** impact the way you share it with others?

6. What are **practical ways** you can model Christ's humility and love in daily life?

7. How can staying connected to **the Vine (John 15:5)** strengthen your ability to love others?

8. When was the last time someone extended grace to you, and how did it impact you?

GRACE JOURNEY TRACKER

Use the tracker below to log your reflections, prayers, and acts of grace:

DATE	ACTS OF GRACE SHOWED	HOW I EXPERIENCE GRACE	AREAS FOR MORE GRACE

Artistic Reflection

Create a visual representation of the overflow of God's grace in your life—perhaps a waterfall, river, or abundant garden.

PERSONAL GROWTH

Reflect on the blessings of God's grace in your life and how they've impacted others. What steps can you take to let His grace overflow even more?

BLESSING

May the grace of God overflow in your life, bringing joy, peace, and transformation. May others be drawn to Christ through the evidence of His grace at work in you.

Session 8

GRACE IN ACTION - LIVING OUT GRACE IN A HOSTILE WORLD

Lesson Objectives

By the end of this lesson, readers should be able to:

- **Recognize the challenges of living out faith in a world that may not understand or accept it.**
- **Develop a Christlike approach to opposition**, responding with grace rather than retaliation.
- **Learn how to engage in difficult conversations about faith**, using wisdom and love.
- **Identify ways to stand firm in their beliefs** while still showing kindness and compassion.
- **Commit to being a light in the world**, living in a way that draws others to Christ.

OPEN

Leader: Open the session with prayer. Ask if there are any questions from the previous session.

Prayer

"Father, show me how to live a life filled with grace. Help me to reflect Your love and compassion even in difficult circumstances. Empower me to stand firm in my faith and be a light in the world. Amen."

Opening Question: "Think of a recent situation where you had the opportunity to extend grace but found it difficult. What made it challenging, and how do you think responding with grace could have changed the outcome?"

Chapter Overview

This chapter explores how grace transforms daily life and empowers believers to live out their faith in a world that is often hostile to Christian values. It focuses on responding to opposition with kindness, integrity, and resilience while staying true to biblical convictions.

Living out our faith in a world that often opposes Christian values requires both courage and grace. This chapter explores how believers can remain steadfast in their faith while responding to opposition with love, patience, and wisdom. It emphasizes that grace is not just something we receive but something we actively demonstrate in our interactions, even with those who challenge us.

Through biblical examples such as Jesus' response to persecution and Paul's endurance in spreading the gospel, this chapter highlights the importance of spiritual resilience. It calls believers to reflect the love of Christ in every situation, showing grace without compromising their convictions.

Key Memory Verse

Matthew 5:14-16 (NLT) – *"You are the light of the world—like a city on a hilltop that cannot be hidden. No one lights a lamp and then puts it under a basket. Instead, a lamp is placed on a stand, where it gives light to everyone in the house. In the same way, let your good deeds shine out for all to see, so that everyone will praise your heavenly Father."*

GROUP DISCUSSION QUESTIONS - *Understanding Grace in Action*

1. What are practical ways to show grace in a hostile or difficult situation?

2. How does living out grace in a hostile world demonstrate Christ's love?

3. What does **Titus 2:11** say about the grace of God and salvation?

4. How does **Colossians 3:12-14** describe the characteristics of a grace-filled life?

5. How does the doctrine of **imago Dei** (image of God) relate to our call to extend grace?

6. In what ways does **2 Corinthians 5:17** emphasize transformation through grace?

7. Why is maintaining **integrity** important when living out grace in a hostile world?

8. What role does the **Holy Spirit** play in equipping believers to extend grace?

9. How can believers **balance faith and professionalism** in secular workplaces?

10. What does **living out grace** look like in response to hostility or opposition?

11. How can we apply **Matthew 5:16** ("Let your light shine before others") in our daily lives?

12. How does Jesus' **response to opposition** teach us to live with grace and conviction?

13. What steps can we take to foster **unity and service** in our communities?

14. How does **grace empower** us to forgive others, even when it's difficult?

15. How does standing firm in truth while showing grace reflect **Christ's character**?

PRACTICAL APPLICATION QUESTIONS

1. How can you embody compassion, kindness, humility, gentleness, and patience in your daily interactions?

2. **Reflect** on a recent situation where you struggled to show grace. How might you handle it differently now?

3. Have you ever struggled with showing grace in a difficult situation? What was the outcome?

4. What are **practical ways** you can demonstrate grace to those who may oppose your faith?

5. What barriers (bitterness, fear, pride) do you need to overcome to live more grace-filled?

6. How can **prayer and scripture** help you cultivate daily practice of grace?

7. Reflect on a moment when you were shown **unexpected grace**. How did it impact you?

GRACE JOURNEY TRACKER

Use the tracker below to log your reflections, prayers, and acts of grace:

DATE	ACTS OF GRACE SHOWED	HOW I EXPERIENCE GRACE	AREAS FOR MORE GRACE

Artistic Reflection

Create a sketch or poem that represents standing firm in grace amidst challenges.

PERSONAL GROWTH

Reflect on how God's grace can transform your response to hostility or adversity. What practical steps can you take to live out grace in your community?

BLESSING

May the grace of God empower you to live boldly and compassionately in a world that often opposes your faith. May you find strength in His love to overcome hostility with kindness and courage to stand firm in truth.

Session 9

EXTENDING GRACE IN WEAKNESS

Lesson Objectives

By the end of this lesson, readers should be able to:

- **Recognize that weakness is not a limitation but an opportunity for God's grace to work.**
- **Understand how to extend grace to themselves and others**, particularly in times of failure or struggle.
- **Develop patience and compassion** for those who are still growing in their faith.
- **Identify personal areas where they need to surrender their weaknesses to God**, allowing His strength to be made perfect.
- **Commit to living with a grace-filled perspective**, seeing themselves and others through God's eyes.

OPEN

Leader: Open the session with prayer. Ask if there are any questions from the previous session.

Prayer

"Jesus, show me how to share Your grace with those around me. Use me as an instrument of Your love and kindness. Give me boldness to speak of Your grace and humility to serve others. Amen."

Opening Question: "Can you think of a time when you felt completely unqualified, weak, or inadequate for something, but somehow God's grace carried you through? How did that experience shape your faith?"

Chapter Overview

God's grace is most powerful when we are at our weakest. This chapter explores how believers are called not only to receive grace but also to extend it—especially in moments of failure, struggle, or brokenness. It emphasizes that showing grace to others, and even to ourselves, is a reflection of God's love and character.

Using Peter's failure and restoration as a key biblical example, the chapter highlights how God does not condemn us in our weakness but instead strengthens and restores us. It also teaches that extending grace requires humility, patience, and reliance on the Holy Spirit.

Key Memory Verse

Isaiah 40:29 (NLT) *"He gives strength to the weary and increases the power of the weak."*

GROUP DISCUSSION QUESTIONS

1. How does recognizing your weaknesses allow God's grace to shine through?

2. What role does grace play in serving and supporting others despite our limitations?

3. What does it mean to extend grace in weakness? How is this principle reflected in both Peter's and Gideon's stories?

4. How does **2 Corinthians 12:10** reframe our understanding of weakness and strength in Christ?

5. Why is grace not only about receiving but also about giving? How does this align with **Matthew 28:19-20** (The Great Commission)?

6. How does **Luke 6:36** emphasize the importance of showing grace and compassion to others?

7. How does Gideon's story in **Judges 6:11-16** illustrate God's ability to use human weakness for His glory?

8. Why do you think weakness is often viewed negatively in society? How does Scripture challenge that perspective?

9. How do you balance showing grace while also upholding biblical truth?

10. In what ways can the church better extend grace to those who feel unworthy or broken?

11. How does the example of the 144,000 in Revelation relate to the call for believers to live in faithfulness and extend grace?

12. How do you respond when someone else's weakness affects you negatively? How can you show grace in those moments?

13. If grace is God's power at work in us, how can we better rely on it when facing personal trials or difficulties?

14. The chapter describes grace as **"a bridge over a chasm of weakness."** How do you interpret this metaphor in your own spiritual journey?

PRACTICAL APPLICATION QUESTIONS

1. **Reflect** on a time when you felt too weak or inadequate. How did God's grace sustain you?

2. What areas do you feel weak in today? Write your own "Peter and David" story, recalling a time you either received grace in weakness or extended grace to someone who needed it and invite God to work through them.

3. **Dependence on Grace:** In what areas of your life do you struggle with self-reliance? How can you shift your focus toward God's sufficiency?

4. **Overcoming Barriers:** What emotional or spiritual barriers keep you from extending grace to others?

5. **Living the Message:** What does it mean to be an "ambassador of grace"? How can you live out this calling in your daily interactions?

6. **Sharing Grace:** Have you ever hesitated to share the gospel out of fear or inadequacy? How does God's promise in **Matthew 28:20** encourage you to be bold in extending grace to the unsaved?

GRACE JOURNEY TRACKER

Use the tracker below to log your reflections, prayers, and acts of grace:

Date	Acts of Grace Showed	How I Experience Grace	Areas for More Grace

Artistic Reflection

Write a poem or draw a symbol that represents how God's grace strengthens you in weakness.

PERSONAL GROWTH

Reflect on how embracing your weaknesses can help you rely more fully on God's strength. What steps will you take to extend grace to others?

Practical Mercy: Think about a situation where you struggled to show mercy. How can embracing your own weaknesses enable you to extend compassion more freely?

Community Impact: How can extending grace create transformation within your family, church, or workplace?

Forgiveness: Is there someone in your life who has wronged you and needs your grace? What steps can you take toward forgiveness and reconciliation?

Write down one practical way they can extend grace this week—whether through forgiveness, service, or sharing the gospel.

"Write a prayer asking for grace in an area of weakness" or "Reflect on how God's grace has transformed your biggest struggles."

Memorization Verse: Memorize 2 Corinthians 12:9-10 to remember that God's grace is made perfect in weakness.

Closing Reflection: "How would your life change if you truly believed that God's grace is sufficient in your weaknesses?"

BLESSING

May the God of all grace strengthen you in your weakness and transform your limitations into platforms for His glory. May His grace empower you to forgive, to serve, and to love, even when you feel inadequate.

$\mathcal{S}ession$ 10
GRACE IN DISCIPLESHIP

Lesson Objectives

By the end of this lesson, readers should be able to:

- **Understand that discipleship is an ongoing process** that requires daily renewal of the mind.
- **Recognize the role of grace in transforming their thoughts, attitudes, and behaviors.**
- **Identify areas in their thinking that need to be aligned with God's truth.**
- **Commit to spiritual disciplines** such as prayer, scripture meditation, and accountability in a faith community.
- **Develop a renewed mindset** that reflects Christ's character and purpose.

OPEN

Leader: Open the session with prayer. Ask if there are any questions from the previous session.

Prayer

"Father, let grace abound in our church community and in sharing the gospel. Unite us in love and purpose and help us to support one another with patience and understanding. Amen."

Opening Question: "Think of a time when someone invested in your spiritual growth—maybe through mentorship, encouragement, or simply walking alongside you in faith. How did their influence shape your relationship with God?"

Chapter Overview

Discipleship is more than just believing in Christ—it is about being transformed by His grace and committing to a lifelong journey of growth. This chapter explores how grace renews the mind, reshaping thoughts, attitudes, and actions to align with God's will. True discipleship requires intentional surrender, obedience, and a willingness to be molded by God.

Using Romans 12:2 as a foundation, this chapter emphasizes that transformation is not about conforming to worldly standards but about allowing God to change how we think and live. It also highlights the importance of surrounding oneself with a Christ-centered community for spiritual accountability and growth.

Key Memory Verse

Romans 12:2 (NLT) – *"Don't copy the behavior and customs of this world, but let God transform you into a new person by changing the way you think. Then you will learn to know God's will for you, which is good and pleasing and perfect."*

GROUP DISCUSSION QUESTIONS – *Deeper Engagement*

1. How does grace shape our approach to discipleship?

2. What are the challenges of extending grace within the church, and how can we overcome them?

3. How does discipleship function as a journey rather than a one-time event?

4. What is the key role of grace in discipleship, and how does it empower spiritual growth?

5. Why is obedience in the life of a believer described as a response to grace rather than an obligation (Romans 12:1-2)?

6. How does **Luke 9:23** emphasize the cost of discipleship, and in what ways does grace help bear this cost?

7. In **John 15:5**, Jesus describes Himself as the vine and believers as the branches. How does this metaphor illustrate the relationship between grace and discipleship?

8. Why is unity in the church important for discipleship, and how does **Ephesians 4:29** encourage believers to use their words for building up rather than tearing down?

9. What does **2 Timothy 2:2** teach about the importance of mentoring and multiplying disciples?

10. How does the Great Commission (**Matthew 28:19-20**) connect to discipleship, and why is making disciples a central part of the Christian faith?

11. How does discipleship help shape not just individuals but entire church communities?

12. Why do you think some believers struggle with sharing their faith or mentoring others? How can grace overcome those fears?

13. What role does accountability play in discipleship, and how does grace help create a safe space for growth?

14. How can the church be more intentional about creating a culture of discipleship that extends beyond the pulpit?

15. The story in this chapter highlighted a church that was transformed through discipleship based on grace. How can churches today create a similar atmosphere of spiritual growth and healing?

16. How does discipleship strengthen faith during difficult seasons of life?

17. What practical steps can a believer take to transition from being a disciple to discipling others?

PRACTICAL APPLICATION QUESTIONS

1. How do you contribute to the unity and peace of your church community?

2. What actions can you take to show grace to someone in your church who may be struggling?

3. How has God's grace transformed your own discipleship journey? What lessons have you learned along the way?

4. In what areas of your life do you feel God is calling you to greater obedience? How can grace empower you to take that next step?

5. The chapter highlights the importance of grace in sustaining faithfulness. When have you experienced God's grace helping you persevere through spiritual struggles?

6. What are some challenges you have faced in mentoring others in their spiritual journey? How can grace help you become a better disciple-maker?

7. Think about a time when you struggled to obey God. What role did grace play in helping you trust Him?

8. What are some specific ways you can reflect Christ's grace within your church community to foster unity and encouragement?

9. Have you ever been on the receiving end of grace in a discipleship setting? How did it impact your spiritual growth?

GRACE JOURNEY TRACKER

Use the tracker below to log your reflections, prayers, and acts of grace:

Date	Acts of Grace Showed	How I Experience Grace	Areas for More Grace

Artistic Reflection

Write a prayer or draw an image that represents unity and grace within the body of Christ.

PERSONAL GROWTH

Reflect on how grace has shaped your involvement in your church or ministry. How can you foster a community of grace and encouragement?

Scripture Reflection: Meditate on **John 15:5, Luke 9:23, and 2 Timothy 2:2**, journaling how these scriptures shape your understanding of discipleship

Discipleship Accountability Partner Challenge: Find an accountability partner for one month to pray for each other and encourage one another in your discipleship journey.

Grace and Discipleship Journal: "Write about a time when you discipled someone or were discipled by someone. How did grace play a role in the experience?"

"List three ways God's grace has helped you remain faithful in your walk with Him."

"Reflect on how your mind has been **transformed** through discipleship. What changes have you noticed in your attitudes, priorities, or behaviors?"

Discipleship in Action: Commit to one action step in your discipleship journey, such as mentoring a new believer, leading a small group, or sharing the gospel with someone.

Grace in Community: Brainstorm ways to encourage and uplift your church community, practicing **Ephesians 4:29** by using words that build up.

Memory Verse Challenge: Memorize **2 Timothy 2:2** as a reminder of your calling to disciple others.

Reflect and Apply: "What practical changes can you make in your daily life to live out the call to discipleship with grace?"

BLESSING

May God's grace empower you to live a life of joyful obedience to His will. May you find peace and purpose in abiding in Christ and bearing fruit for His glory.

$Session$ 11
ETERNAL IMPACT OF GRACE

Lesson Objectives

By the end of this lesson, readers should be able to:

- **Understand that grace has an eternal impact**, shaping both their destiny and their influence on others.
- **Recognize the importance of living with an eternal perspective**, focusing on what truly matters.
- **Identify ways they can invest in their spiritual legacy**, impacting others through discipleship and evangelism.
- **Develop a mindset that sees beyond temporary struggles**, trusting in God's greater plan.
- **Commit to living in a way that reflects God's eternal grace**, influencing others for Christ.

<u>OPEN</u>

Leader: Open the session with prayer. Ask if there are any questions from the previous session.

Prayer

"Lord, thank You for the grace that sustains me through every season of life. Keep me rooted in Your love and faithful in prayer. May my journey be a testament to the enduring power of Your grace. Amen."

Opening Question: "If your life were a letter of grace written to the world, what would it say? How would your words, actions, and faith leave a lasting imprint on those around you?"

Chapter Overview

Grace is not just for the present—it has an eternal impact. This chapter explores how the grace we receive transforms our destiny, giving us the assurance of eternal life and the opportunity to leave a lasting spiritual legacy. It emphasizes that believers are called to live with an eternal perspective, knowing that their faithfulness on earth has rewards in eternity.

Through 2 Corinthians 4:17-18, the chapter encourages believers to focus on things that have eternal value rather than temporary struggles. It also highlights how sharing grace with others—through discipleship, evangelism, and a Christ-centered life—can impact future generations.

Key Memory Verse

2 Corinthians 4:17-18 (NLT) – *"For our present troubles are small and won't last very long. Yet they produce for us a glory that vastly outweighs them and will last forever! So we don't look at the troubles we can see now; rather, we fix our gaze on things that cannot be seen. For the things we see now will soon be gone, but the things we cannot see will last forever."*

GROUP DISCUSSION QUESTIONS

1. How does understanding the eternal impact of grace influence the way we live today?

2. In what ways can we share the message of eternal grace with others?

3. How does God's grace sustain believers beyond salvation and into daily life?

4. What does **Matthew 5:16** teach about the role of grace in influencing others?

5. How does Margaret's story illustrate the idea that grace leaves a lasting legacy?

6. Why is the feeding of the 5,000 (John 6:1-14) a powerful illustration of God's overflowing grace?

7. What does **Revelation 21:6** reveal about the eternal nature of grace?

8. How does God's covenant (**Lamentations 3:22-23**) assure believers that grace will never fail?

9. What does **Hebrews 4:16** mean when it invites us to approach the "throne of grace" boldly?

10. In what ways does grace encourage believers to live with an eternal perspective?

11. What is the connection between grace and **Ephesians 3:20-21**, which speaks of God accomplishing more than we can ask or imagine?

12. How does grace transform barren areas of life into flourishing places of faith and purpose?

13. How can grace inspire acts of service and generosity that leave a lasting impact?

14. Why is it important to focus on the **long-term impact of grace**, rather than just immediate results?

15. What are the dangers of taking grace for granted?

16. How does living with an eternal mindset change the way believers handle challenges, relationships, and responsibilities?

17. The story of Margaret demonstrates how grace multiplies over generations. What are some ways we can pass down the legacy of grace to our families and communities?

18. What does it mean to approach the "throne of grace" confidently, and how can this impact your prayer life?

19. In what ways can the church foster a culture of grace that extends beyond its members and into the community?

20. How does grace help us to reconcile relationships and heal wounds that might otherwise cause division?

21. The feeding of the 5,000 shows how God multiplies even the smallest offerings. How can we apply this principle when serving others?

22. What steps can we take to ensure that we are **not just recipients of grace, but also distributors of grace**?

PRACTICAL APPLICATION QUESTIONS

1. Think about a difficult season in your life. How did God's grace sustain you?

2. Reflect on the hope and assurance that grace gives you, knowing that it will lead you to the fulfillment of God's promises in eternity.

3. How has God's grace sustained you during a difficult season?

4. Reflect on a time when you felt inadequate but saw God's grace provide what you needed.

5. How does knowing that God's grace is eternal change the way you live your daily life?

6. How does the assurance of grace affect how you handle stress, worry, or uncertainty?

7. How can you be more intentional about allowing grace to shape your decisions and interactions with others?

8. In what ways has grace given you strength to persevere through a personal struggle?

9. Think of a time when someone extended grace to you. How did it impact your view of God's love?

10. How does an eternal perspective help you show more grace and patience toward others?

11. What areas of your life do you need to surrender so that God's grace can overflow into them?

12. What are some practical ways you can ensure that your legacy is one of grace?

GRACE JOURNEY TRACKER

Use the tracker below to log your reflections, prayers, and acts of grace:

Date	Acts of Grace Showed	How I Experience Grace	Areas for More Grace

Artistic Reflection

Create an illustration or write a story that symbolizes the eternal nature of God's grace.

PERSONAL GROWTH

Write a **"Grace Legacy Letter"** to someone—a friend, child, or mentee—sharing how God's grace has changed their life and how they hope to pass it on. This could be a **testimony of faith** or even **words of encouragement** to leave behind as a spiritual legacy.

Reflect on God's enduring grace throughout your life. What lessons have you learned, and how will you live with an eternal perspective moving forward?

Reflect and Apply: *How can you ensure that your life reflects the grace of God in a way that impacts eternity?*

Identify three ways you can make grace a more active force in your life.

Memorize **Hebrews 4:16** as a reminder of God's invitation to approach Him boldly.

Eternal Perspective Journal: Write about **how grace has impacted your past, present, and future**.

Prayer of Surrender Exercise: Write a **personal prayer surrendering an area of your life where you need to trust God's grace** more fully.

The Legacy of Grace Challenge: Identify **one way you can pass grace forward**—whether through a small act of kindness, mentorship, or sharing your testimony.

Grace in Action Commitment: Commit to one practical act of grace this week, whether through forgiveness, generosity, encouragement, or service.

Scripture Meditation Activity: Meditate on key verses such as **Hebrews 4:16, Ephesians 3:20-21, and Revelation 21:6**.

Grace-Focused Testimony Night/Day: Share a **personal story of how grace has changed your lives** with your study group.

Imagining Heaven: Reflect on the eternal nature of grace and write a letter to your future self about how you want grace to shape your legacy.

BLESSING

May the overflowing grace of God touch every part of your life. May His love fill you to the point that it spills over and blesses everyone you meet. May you experience the eternal impact of God's grace every day.

FINAL COMMISSIONING PRAYER

"Lord, as we conclude this journey, we ask that Your grace never stop flowing in and through us. May we be vessels of Your love, reflections of Your mercy, and voices of hope in a world that desperately needs Your grace. Help us to pass this gift to others, leaving a legacy of faith that glorifies You. In Jesus' name, Amen."

BONUS MATERIALS

Grace in Different Contexts

Family Life

- Reflect on how you can show grace to your spouse, children, or parents.

Workplace

- Consider ways to model grace through your actions and words.

Community Service

- Look for opportunities to serve others with a heart of grace.

Evangelism

- Share the message of grace through conversations and actions.

Prayers for Special Circumstances

- **Grace in Conflict Resolution**: "Lord, help me to approach conflict with humility and grace. Give me the wisdom to listen, the courage to speak truth in love, and the patience to seek reconciliation."
- **Grace During Personal Failure**: "Father, I thank You that Your grace is sufficient even in my failures. Help me to trust in Your forgiveness and to learn from my mistakes."
- **Grace to Forgive Oneself or Others**: "Jesus, You have forgiven me so much. Help me to extend that same grace to myself and those who have hurt me."

- **Grace in Leadership or Mentorship**: "Lord, guide me as I lead and mentor others. May Your grace shape my actions and words, reflecting Your love and truth."

Key Insight:

Grace is foundational to our lives—it is not something we work for, but something we receive. Embracing this frees us from feelings of inadequacy or self-righteousness, knowing that God's love for us isn't based on our performance.

Grace doesn't eliminate our struggles, but it equips us to endure them. This verse invites us to embrace our weaknesses, knowing that it is in these moments that God's grace is revealed in its full power.

Grace leads us to live a transformed life—not through sheer willpower, but through the work of the Holy Spirit. As we experience grace, our desires change, and we grow toward greater holiness and integrity.

Grace is boundless. The more we recognize the depth of our sin, the greater we see the depth of God's grace. His grace covers and redeems us, no matter how great the sin.

God's throne is not a place of judgment, but of grace. We are invited to come as we are, knowing that His mercy will meet our needs and empower us to live according to His will.

Glossary of Theological Terms

Sanctification: The process of being made holy through the work of the Holy Spirit.

Justification: The act of God declaring a sinner righteous through faith in Christ.

Imago Dei: Latin for 'Image of God,' reflecting our creation in God's likeness.

CERTIFICATE OF COMPLETION

This certifies that _____ has
completed the "'**Changed by His Amazing Grace** " workbook, deepening
their understanding and application of God's transformative grace.

Date: _____

Signature: _____